The wonderful lives of

WHALES

Written and Illustrated by

FRANK DAPPAH

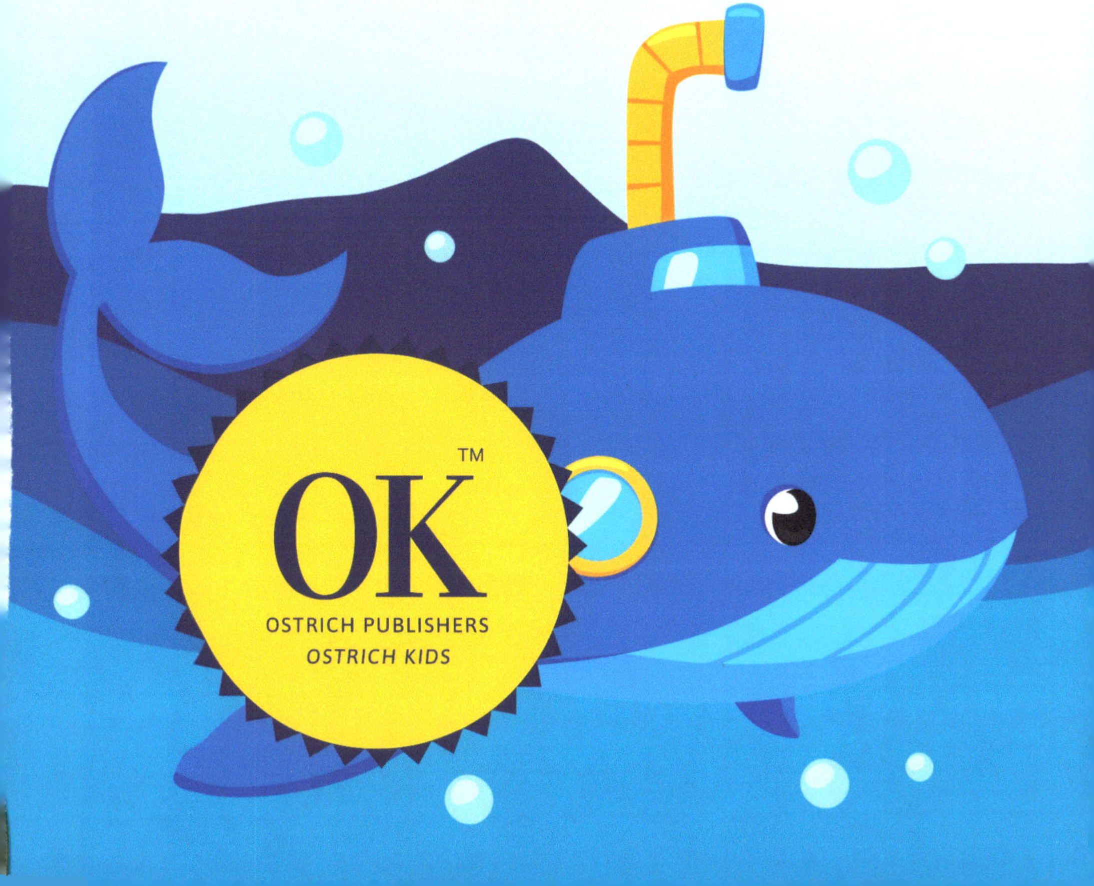

OK™
OSTRICH PUBLISHERS
OSTRICH KIDS

A Whale is not a fish

Whales are mammals. This means they breathe air, have hair and the females produce milk to feed their babies.

Sperm whale

There she blows!

Since whales breath air, unlike fish, they breathe through nostrils, called a blowhole, located right on top of their heads.

Orca

Baleen on me when you are not strong

Baleen Whales and Toothed Whales are both types of whales.

Big blue

The Blue Whale is the biggest animal to ever live with the largest coming in at 418,878 pounds. That's like 10 Elephants.

Blue Whales

Sing me a song

Most whales make moaning sounds but Humpback whales, Blue whales, and a few others sing.

Dinner time

Baleen whales eat mostly plankton and krill (tiny ocean creatures similar to shrimp).

Only Half-Sleep

Whales sleep by shutting down only half of their brain for rest. This way, the other half can make sure they take breaths when needed.

A Pod of life

Most whales move in groups called pods. Pods can be as small as two whales and be as big as hundred or more whales.

OTHER BOOKS

THE SKY
UP THERE
Written & Illustrated by
Frank dappah
OK
OSTRICH PUBLISHERS
OSTRICH KIDS

GATHONI NJENGA
CURIOSITY ONLY KILLS
CATS
OK
OSTRICH PUBLISHERS
OSTRICH KIDS

BUILD
SOMETHING
Written and Illustrated by Frank Dappah
OK
OSTRICH PUBLISHERS
OSTRICH KIDS

HATARI'S
SHADOW
Written by Gathoni Njenga